What Happened Was...

What Happened Was. . .

ON WRITING PERSONAL ESSAY AND MEMOIR

Genie Zeiger

WHITE PINE PRESS / BUFFALO, NEW YORK

WHITE PINE PRESS
P.O. BOX 236
BUFFALO, NEW YORK 14201

With thanks to *The Sun,* in which these essays first appeared:
"20, 40, 60, 80," July 2005, Issue 355
"O My Little Breath," August, 2001, Issue 308
"Mezuzah," April 2001, Issue 304
"At My Bedroom Window," November 1999, Issue 287

"20, 40, 60, 80" also appeared in *The Best American Siritual Writing 2006,*
ed. Philip Zaleski, Houghton Mifflin Co.

Cover painting by Paris street artist Yaseen Khan.

Publication of this book was made possible, in part, with public
funds from the New York State Council on the Arts, a State Agency.

First Edition.

ISBN: 978-1-9352109-04-7

Printed and bound in the United States of America.

Library of Congress Control Number: 2009921874

For
Sy Safransky
editor of The Sun,
without whose encouragement
these essays would not
have escaped my notebooks.

Contents

What Happened Was...

Everyday we have more stories, "what happened was's.." that accrue and make for what we call "a life." In telling our stories, we make connections between events and self and thereby come to understand our lives, why we are here. As we tell our stories, and far more profoundly as we write them, the lens changes and we see more deeply, we unveil mystery with words.

How to begin? How does one choose from the enormity of feelings and thoughts, memories and dreams; how does one choose what to say, and how does one say it on the page? Ironically, thought, (often the premier dictator with regard to expression), is somewhat useless because writing about your life means, essentially, letting your life write itself. Your best guide in finding the stories most essential to you is your pen. As one six-teen-year-old student of mine said, "You gotta let your pen talk," which means bypassing reason and allowing the unconscious, imagination to whisper in your ear.

Writing is feeling a self, confronting a self, coming closer to what it is inside us that wants to greet and know us. Because these aspects of ourselves are often hidden, exposing them may threaten our habitual idea of who we think we are. Therefore, we put off writing—we clean the house, pick up the phone, Google "post-nasal drip."

We each have unique personal histories, stories to tell—funny ones, profound ones, tragic ones. Embedded in our stories are our own truths which, if deeply excavated, turn out to be those of others as well. Here's what the writer Barry Lopez has to say in his book, *Crow and Weasel* (North Point Press, 1990):

> I would ask you to remember this
> one thing," said Badger. "The sto-

ries people tell have a way of taking care of them. If stories come to you, care for them. And learn to give them away where they are needed. Sometimes a person needs a story more than food to stay alive. This is why we put stories in each other's memory. This is how people take care of themselves...

Which stories matter enough to be told? In his essay, "100 False Starts" in the March 4, 1933 issue of *The Saturday Evening Post*, F. Scott Fitzgerald wrote the following: (Suggestion: As you read this excerpt, be aware of the use of verbs and the repetition of one in particular.)

Mostly, we authors repeat ourselves—that's the truth. We have two or three great and moving experiences in our lives—experiences so great and so moving that it doesn't seem at the time that anyone else has been so caught up and pounded and dazzled and astonished and beaten and broken and rescued and illuminated and illuminated and rewarded and humbled in just that way ever before.

Then we learn our trade, well or less well, and we tell our two or three stories—each time in a new disguise—maybe ten times, maybe one hundred, as long as people will listen.

With the personal essay, a more discrete event or linked series of events is revealed; with memoir a longer period of one's life is explored. In both cases, one starts with memory, "what happened was...."

THE PERSONAL ESSAY

Unlike the formal essay, the personal essay is most often shorter, and typically relies upon imaginative leaps more akin to that of the poet than to the biographer or journalist. You may, perhaps, be writing about your mother, about how she always burned the string beans, or about her strong moral character, and then suddenly you remember how she insisted that you carry that orange and black UNICEF box along with your paper grocery bag for candy on Halloween. This rumination may then lead you to thoughts about your own sense of right and wrong, of some current moral dilemma and so the narrative follows. It is not a straight line, but a curving one drawn forward by an inner guide, and the more you befriend that guide, i.e., write, the easier the process of writing becomes.

As you put pen to paper, you may find yourself weaving what initially reads like a disparate stream of situations and characters. If you follow what John Gardner, the novelist called in his book, *The Art of Fiction*, (Alfred A. Knopf, 1984) "the narrative dream," the innate associative powers of the imagination, you'll find that what you write represents reality far more than what you believe is your "real life." And so, when writing about one thing, welcome the odd thought, the alien idea that comes slantwise taking you in a direction you never had in mind. Allow this process again and again and you'll find in the end that somehow you've constructed a whole.

Memory is never objective or reliable. We re-create the past with words, words which form images resulting from the marriage of language and imagination. You may remember, for example, that your father smoked Camels, (or were they Pall Mall's? It doesn't matter), and you write, "My father smoked..." As you continue, you see that old ceramic cigarette case with the deer painted in gold on the lid, you see the mahogany coffee table upon which that cigarette holder sat. A feeling comes over you, and you sense the long hallway of the house you grew up in, the atmosphere—loneliness, perhaps, or safety, and you allow your words to be infused by these feeling tones as you linger in those rooms. You keep at your writing and in so doing you re-create a past that is real and alive. There is no other.

Telling our stories, making sense of our lives

through language, creates a self. When you write about the difficulties, the inexplicable parts of your life, you become able to untangle them and often arrive at a deeper understanding of who you truly are. With this process, you are made more whole, closer to spirit, to whichever God or sense of holiness is your own. There is a Jewish belief that when God created this world, divine unity became scattered into holy sparks, which remain hidden everywhere. It is our job to do *"tikkun olam,"* repair of the world, which includes repair of ourselves, by gathering these sparks, to make whole that which was broken. As a writing workshop leader for twenty years, I see that the pieces of the stories we need to tell are often composed of those scattered sparks; we unearth them and mold them into story and as our stories become whole, so with us.

When you write from where your excitement arises, where the energy pulsates, you will find that it originates in the unfinished parts of the self—the disquieting, undigested parts. You gather the words, line them up to embrace them, and yourself.

In our day-to-day lives, we are repeatedly asked, "How 'ya doing?" and, often, behind the reflexive, "I'm fine, how are you?" lie other words. We are compelled to write what we have little place to say, the hard stuff, the neglected feelings.

Happiness is its own completion—try describing your happiness and you'll find it enormously difficult to get beyond cliché. (You are far better off singing!) Sometimes we fear telling the hard truth because we don't want to burden others, but the telling is often a gift to others, as well as to the self. I am not talking "whining" here, I'm talking truth-telling.

"There is another world, but the only way to it is through this one," wrote the French poet Paul Valery, i.e., the writer takes us to the other world, the one beyond the self, through the self. This is why writing is a sacred act, a meditation, a prayer.

What calls you to that other world, what wants you to see and know it, no matter how it manifests, must be honored: staring at a particular tree, a particular sky; watching the mentally ill man, sunburned and scruffy, outside the café; overhearing others talk; playing with a child. In summary, we must embrace whatever calls to us and then translate our experience into language. When we do so, feeling and revelation become a form of love.

An excellent warm up exercise for writing is quite simple. Sit yourself down, pick up your pen, have a clock nearby and write the words, "I remember…" then free write for five minutes, i.e., let your pen, not your conscious mind, lead the way. Stop for a few seconds and then write, "I don't remember…" for five minutes. Switch back and forth, five minutes for each pass, three times. After you've completed this process, read all you have written and look for the "hot spots," images and stories which ignite your consciousness and therefore call you back for more: Here is one of my experiences with this particular prompt:

> I remember being born… no, that's
> not true. I remember waving to my
> mother after she waved to me, her
> hand like a small white flag as she

sat at the window at Kings Highway Hospital after having given birth to my sister. I remember calling it the Kings Highway Veterinary Hospital to bug my sister when we were older, and I knew what a veterinary hospital actually was. I remember her asthmatic breathing, the palpable terror in our shared little bedroom, how much I wanted out of there as I listened to her, how I wished she would stop breathing. But then she'd die. Sometimes I wished she would die...

I don't remember my Dad or the living room where he danced with my Mom—the hi-fi in the corner on its four wrought iron legs, its cream colored veneer. Nor do I remember how Mom and Dad, who rarely spoke, fox trotted on the beautiful Chinese rug with flowers that bumped up, how Sinatra crooned in the background, how I watched and saw the emblem of a husband and wife.

I remember Sarah, who is she? I don't know. I remember Carl, two Carl's—a father Carl and a husband Carl, how I fell for the second one, the first boyfriend in my life. I don't remember when I first hugged him, kissed him beside that aqua pool at the country club, how my body seemed to explode—it was wondrous, I remember, looking back that I could have been Juliet and he Romeo, I could have been Isolde, and he Tristan...

I don't remember yelling loudly at each other in that apartment in Queens, jets from Kennedy blaring in the background and two beautiful children running around making messes, my blind devotion to them blinding me from seeing my real unhappiness with my Dad—I meant to write "husband." Huh? What's that about? I know. I don't want to know.

In this exercise, I excavated themes that have been at the center of my life—birth, siblings, parenting, falling in and out of love.

I urge writers to spend some time each day pen in hand. Often this writing will feel trivial, uninteresting. Often it will be simply a way of sweeping away the pedestrian stuff of what happens in order to make space for the deeper stories. But often a phrase, a line, the seed of a story will arise with daily practice. Note it, mark it, highlight it, save it and go back to it.

A nasty, pervasive character with whom you will be forced to deal as you continue your writing practice is the inner critic. My own, like yours most likely, was born in my parents' home and in school. In truth, however, my particular inner critic had a comparatively short shelf life because I became so taken with, so enamored of and consumed by the written word. This love began early when, as a child, I simply could not read enough. The love of reading led, inexorably to the love of writing. This is true of most writers. And speaking of stages of life, I've come to see that there are two kinds of writers: those who begin early and never stop, and those who need to accrue enough life experience to feel ready to begin. I fit in the latter category for although I wrote some in diaries, journals, and produced an occasional poem, I did not really begin to write until I was almost forty. Now, at age sixty-five, I have six books with my name on their covers, but I say, in all truth, that their presence is far outweighed by the simple joy I often feel when lining up words on the page and then laboring to make them work just right.

I write because I have to. I write to experience

what I experience for the second time and, in so doing, to better understand myself, the world and my place in it. I write to reveal the self that resides in a higher place than the one in which my mind usually takes up residence. I write because I love words and books because they were the real world—a world of passion and victory and loss and romance for me when, as a child, I was stuck in the silent paralysis of the fifties. I also write because, as I've come to understand, it is my gift, and if you don't open, use, share your gift, it dies. I write because it is my most honest devotional act, the act of questioning and, thankfully, answers often come in words dressed in finery or rags. To be more specific, I find consistently that when something is calling to me, troubling me, asking to be understood, the written word often reveals the answer. Again, the pen is a light.

This is an entirely mysterious process, but having experienced it again and again, I've learned to trust and honor it. I have seen people utterly transformed by the act of writing. J., a woman in one of my writing workshops, arrived stooped over and "misbegotten." She began writing and as she read aloud I found that I had no idea what she was writing about—it was cryptic beyond measure. After a number of weeks, I suggested we meet. We sat side by side in the sun on the deck behind my house and J. told me of her history of sexual abuse and I told her that she must tell her story, that the writing workshop I was leading was a safe place in which to do so, that I'd support her. She did tell her story, her posture changed, her entire being changed, she went to graduate school and now, instead of waitressing, she is a professor of writing at a local college.

Writing saves lives. With truly traumatic life stories, a safe and nurturing writing group is essential. There is a tribal sense of safety in such a group. I doubt that J. could have accomplished her writing without the presence, the bearing witness by others. I strongly advocate joining a supportive writing workshop, particularly when beginning to write, no matter what your subject. And again, understand that the best critique of your writing is rooted in the encouragement for you to keep on with it. Far too many would-be writers have been silenced by insensitive teachers. One such person who came to my workshop was accused of plagiarizing an essay while in high school. This accusation silenced her for twenty-five years.

As you continue with your writing you will move on past the initial draft or two and require either a trusted, experienced reader or a professional editor. When you reach the point at which you are ready to send work out for publication, you must acquire a coat of armor as most often, particularly at the beginning of this process, you will be met by rejection. Do not agonize over rejections. (I have a very fat folder full of them.) Remember that a rejection slip reflects the opinion of only one person, maybe two, not that of the world,

Most magazines and journals are besieged by your fellow writers also wanting their words to reach others. The competition has gotten stronger in the past decade with the proliferation of MFA programs and the use of computers. As important and satisfying it is to see your work published, simply having it heard by others is part of the process of writing, in some sense a form of completion. Even if you are rejected repeatedly, keep trying. Even if you never send anything out, read your work to whomever will listen. (Be sure she is of an encouraging nature and tie her to a chair if necessary.) Do not agonize about your audience-—write for yourself, not with an audience in mind unless you are writing on assignment

Although we do write to communicate with others, the true lifeblood of writing is communication with Self. Write from the deepest place you can find, write out of the urge to close the gap between you and your true self, and finally between you and others.

Over time I've come to see that I have a relationship with my writing, the way I do with my husband and with people in my life—close and nurturing can, temporarily, turn to distant and, well, lousy, for a while. After having devoted myself to writing for long enough, I know that when my writing and I are not getting along, we'll eventually make up. We always do. Also, like many devotees of the writing process, I tend to love best the last thing I've written. My antidote to this enamored state is to put the piece away so as to come back to it later with clearer vision. Sometimes I'll change from the usual font in which I write, offering me even more distance as I read yet another draft. We each have, or will develop, our own writing process. I start in with a particular notebook, only that notebook, and with the same brand of pen, only that pen. As you continue your writing process, you will unearth your own idiosyncratic routines. Be true to them.

Memoir

Most memoirs are prompted by "getting through." Just check the bestseller list and see how many memoirs are being published and the major themes they embody. Memoirs are now certainly "in." It seems to me that they serve to fill emotional gaps caused by the growing absence of community, the historical movement from storytelling to instant text messaging.

Most first novels are clearly memoirs in disguise because one is compelled to write one's own story before writing that of others. With memoir, you must rely on memory, one of a writer's most powerful tools and one of the most unreliable. As you enter your past, you open a door and you will find that new memories surface: you see the old chair your grandfather sat in, how the light entered that third floor apartment with the wide boulevard outside.

There is no absolute past, only the one we remember, which is rooted in feeling, not in chronology. Chronology may be a useful tool in terms of structure, but one must rely upon feeling, not presumed fact, to move your writing forward because when it comes to memory, there is no "factual" source. Every family member comes from a different family; no two siblings have the same parents.

The serious writer of memoir takes us to a part of her past which was unusually transformative and emotionally charged—a death, abuse, divorce, war. I have seen that it often takes a good ten years after such experiences before one is ready to wrestle it into words. This was true for me in terms of writing about my son's ill-fated trip to Peru in which his friend was murdered and he almost so, as well as about a failed ten-year marriage. Confronting on paper, say, the death of a sibling, the betrayal by a husband, a clinical depression, a stroke of misfortune means digesting the experience and moving on, means sharing that experience and helping others do the same. The particular, related in truth, becomes the universal.

As we age, people tend to be more strongly drawn to telling their stories. Elders often want to chronicle what life was for them, to preserve it for their children, for the future. Each person's story will be influenced not only by unique personal experience, but also by the age in which he has lived. Again, do not worry about "accuracy" as there is no such thing when it comes to memoir. Allow your heart to lead the way.

Another issue the writer of memoir, as well as the writer of personal essay, faces is that of the fear of hurting those about whom one writes, family members in particular. This is one of the most daunting aspect of personal writing and one that each individual writer must come to terms with in her own way. I have gone from using a pen name to protect my daughter, to telling some true but "not nice" things about an ex-husband who reacted poorly, then forgave me. Happily, people will often not recognize themselves in your writing, although to you the description is so clearly "them." Defense mechanisms abound, as does forgiveness. This difficult issue is, I repeat, one which you must grapple with on your own terms.

I have written two memoirs, *How I Find Her: A Mother's Dying and a Daughter's Life,* (Sherman Asher Publishing, 2001) and *Atta Girl!* (Sherman Asher Publishing, 2005). With the former, I recorded in detail my mother's long decline with Parkinson's disease and dementia. As we were very close, this process was often difficult, sometimes agonizing for me. Each week, at my workshop, I chronicled the latest installment of this process. I recorded all my feelings—grief, anger, impatience, guilt. After my mother passed on and an agent became interested in the story, she pointed out that the work needed an "arc," which had to include material about my mother's life prior to her disease. I therefore did some family research, talked to my sister and others, and inserted pictures of her strong young self toward the beginning of the memoir. Because I did not shy away from "the hard stuff," many women have gotten in touch with me and thanked me for helping them to feel less lonely with the myriad of feelings they experienced with their own mothers' dying process. *Atta Girl!* arose of itself, the voice of a young girl bearing a great deal of resemblance to me, talking on the page about her confusion as to what life is all about. I laughed a lot as I wrote in her voice, which was antidote, was a gift that came of itself between the tearful writing about my Mom.

In conclusion, I must reiterate the most widely dispensed advice given to new writers—slow down and use as many concrete sensory details as possible to allow your reader to see, taste, smell, feel, hear and touch what you have. Most importantly, enjoy the excitement of discovering your own creativity, your own truth. You may find yourself laughing, you may find yourself crying. And please, please do not concern yourself with the foolish idea that writing about the self is egotistical. When we are brave enough to plumb the truth of our own existence, it will invariably resonate with the truth of others. And finally, for heaven's sake, carry a small notepad around with you to jot down ideas, words, images so they don't get lost between the items on your shopping list.

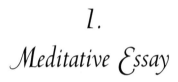

1.

Meditative Essay

One night I couldn't sleep and so I got out of bed and stared for a long time out the living room window. The next day, I recorded what I recalled.

PROMPT: Read "At My Bedroom Window" and then write an personal essay in which little happens but the movement of thought through the mind. Choose a particular place, a particular time of day, whatever external environment invites the internal environment to speak. Allow the movement to be entirely associative, replicating the random nature of the mind's habits. Early morning and dusk are good times for such rumination as the curtains between the two worlds are thinnest at these times.

At My Bedroom Window

I'm awake. Beside me in bed, Bill is wheezing oddly. They say it's the white-pine pollen making a lot of people miserable this spring. There is a gold dusting of it on every surface in the house, as fine as the talc I patted on my kids' bodies ages ago.

I can't get back to sleep. My husband's breathing has conjured up memories of my asthmatic sister lying in the bed beside mine, her small dome of a chest rising and falling with effort. I get up, go downstairs, and pull the hassock of my father's old club chair over to the window to sit. The moon is rising in the east behind a pattern of clouds that looks like the sea, just above the dark, whale-like shape of the house next door. We rarely see these neighbors, but we know that Jean has some kind of cancer, and Dick, a retired state trooper, raises vegetables and beagles: he's recently been sighted naked in his garden, hoe in hand. When Jean is in remission, they take trips, packing their belongings into the huge RV hunched in their driveway, its ungainly beige body a constant reminder that there are significant places on earth beyond our hill, with its quiet beauty.

I've been swimming in another neighbor's pond lately, taking quick plunges into cold water as an act of resistance against advancing middle age. The pond is part of a small Eden that the owners visit on weekends: all solitude and trees and still water (in which I swim with my mouth clamped shut, afraid I might get infected with giardia, as happened ten years ago in Ireland). As I knifed into the pond the other day, thousands of tadpoles scattered on all sides; the cold was delicious on my naked skin.

The night sky outside my window is so watery I want to backstroke into it, sink beneath its silver-flecked surface. I am sad and it is beautiful; in this, we make a good marriage. I imagine my parents up there now. Sometimes I miss them so much I'd do anything to have them back. I keep a large color photo of them on my bureau so they can watch me dress and undress every day. I no longer care if my father sees me naked.

As I stare hungrily at the sky, my daughter is asleep on a mattress on the floor of her apartment in a nearby town. I picture her brown curls on an off-white pillow. Tomorrow she will take a boat down the Connecticut River to study the habitat of bank swallows. My son is asleep beside his fiancée in a fancy townhouse in Washington, D.C. In the morning, he will try to raise more money for the Smithsonian's folk-life center. We are spread out, this family of mine, scattered, no longer under each other's thumbs, although in my mind's eye I can still see the distinctive shape of each of my kids' fingers, how their nails are curved, their particular skin tone, how sunlight colors their hair. I see my daughter, at the age of three, sitting on the toilet in the bathroom of our first house, her legs tight against the sides of the porcelain bowl, as if it were a great white horse. I can see the blond hairs on my dad's fingers, in the spaces between the knuckles and the joints. I remember the exact shape of my mother's ring finger, and the thick gold band she wore there.

When I was young, I stood at my bedroom window and gazed at the highway outside our apartment building, praying to get away from the parents I now want so badly to see. I wanted out of our small, tidy apartment with the rattling mahogany breakfront and its silly cup-and-saucer sets; with the neighbors above and below and on either side; with my tiny room and its brown bed-spread, Formica desk, and gooseneck lamp. Life was elsewhere, and I was so hungry for it I some-times cried. I especially wanted Ricky Flaster to look at me as we rode the bus home from school, to study me as carefully as I studied every night the hundreds of car lights moving below my win-dow, red to the left, white to the right. My skin was too tight, my face too clean, the room behind me too small, my parents too small-minded, my desire too monstrous.

For years, I've collected two things: small stones, some of which sit in a little circle on my desk; and postcards with pictures of roads moving toward the horizon, upon which sits a mountain, a body of water, a house. I tidy up my own home, as if the removal and ordering of everyday objects—papers, shoes, clothing, plates, books—were an act of sanctification, a clearing of some original road home.

Home. The word is home: a little exhalation for the h, then the open o and the yummy m. So like the sacred *om* believed by some to be the sound of God's name, but that initial h humanizes it, graces it with a mild sadness that makes it my own.

When I was nineteen and newly married, I went to Israel. It was summer, and we were to live on a kibbutz for a month. As I descended the metal ramp from the plane into the hot Middle Eastern sun, I found myself pulled by spirit to the hot tarmac. Shy though I was, I got down on my knees, my lips almost pressed to the ground. It wasn't that I was religious—I was not—but rather I was overcome by an inexpressible sense of belonging. This was holy ground, the cause of so much trouble. The tangled blood knot of my soul's yearning unraveled then, and I briefly fit into that alien landscape like the missing piece of a puzzle at last found and set in place.

The clouds have thickened, but I still see their edges rippling. I'm tired, my eyes burn, and I have a lot to do tomorrow. I hear Bill's cough, the sound of his footsteps, the flush of the toilet, then more coughing. Here we are, in this house on a hill, and I have no idea why. At the beginning of this century, my four grandparents crossed the Atlantic to get here from Russia, Poland, and Austria. My parents grew up in New York City, and so did I. Then I moved to the country when I had kids, and that's as far as logic gets me. One of my grandfathers, a good man, was a devout Jew. I doubt he felt this sort of yearning. I imagine his devotion confined his desires.

Now I am here with the sky and less and less time. I hold the world like a glass marble, the kind another neighbor of mine is known for making: a spiral of indigo, a bit or two of red, gold flecks floating in a ball of glass. I want to put this small world, this replica of home, into my mouth, swallow it, die, and be reborn for more. Sometimes I want God so badly I can almost cry, and I confuse

God with the parents I loved, then found small and dull, then lost. And so I carry the sea-sky back into bed with me, in the darkness behind my eyes. I slip under the covers beside Bill and touch his back. Then I roll over, away from him, and curl into a ball, a small world that always wants.

2.
The List

Think of two opposing times, experiences, people, or…. and imaginatively contrast them. This idea came to me as I was looking at all the types of yogurt now available in supermarkets and remembered when "yogurt'" was a word I'd never heard.

PROMPT: Read "Now and Then" and then write a personal essay which is, in essence, a list. It may be a contrasting list, as in "Now and Then," or it could take many other forms. Some I have used are: "A Partial Inventory of My Great Mistakes" another is a list of my experiences with the element of water, which were arranged chronologically, i.e., beginning with my fear of the ocean as a little girl to my fear watching my own kids play in it and wanting desperately to run and in and retrieve them, knowing all the while that I had to allow them their freedom.

Now and Then

Back then, we carried brown paper supermarket bags filled with trash down the dark apartment-house steps to the incinerator, pulled a handle, dumped the bag onto a metal lip, and let go. Now we drive three miles to the town dump to recycle glass, plastic, and paper in clear, twist-tied bags, a yellow Town of Shelburne sticker stuck to the side of each one.

Now we sit outside at night and watch the sky: stars, satellites, planets, meteors, the reliable moon, the Milky Way. Then I'd sneak past Mrs. Ross's apartment and up the stairs piled with her discarded *New York Posts* to the forbidden rooftop, where I'd creep like a spy over the tarry surface, lean against the stained brick chimney, and look up. Then I heard traffic and planes. Now I hear animals and insects—and planes still, but much higher in the sky, on their way to Manchester or Boston.

Then we crouched under desks during air-raid

drills, our hands clasped behind our necks, in fear of the Russians. Now we go about our business, vaguely afraid of vague terrorists, hearing bad news on NPR, war after war perpetuated in our names, and in the name of democracy, and in the name of God.

Then we had 33s, 78s, 45s, and I sang along to the Everly Brothers, Nat King Cole, Frank Sinatra. I danced the twist with my mother to Chubby Checker until the tchotchkes in the breakfront rattled. Now I sing along to CDs. Then I listened to the Beatles sing "Here, There and Everywhere." Now I listen to world music, show tunes, folk, jazz, soul—and the Beatles, still.

Then orange juice was made from frozen concentrate, and my mother mixed it and thrust a glass of it in front of me first thing every morning. Now orange juice comes in waxed cartons, with pulp or without pulp (or with some pulp), with or without calcium and vitamin D, low in acid, from concentrate or freshly squeezed. Then we ate salami, pastrami, tongue. Now we eat yogurt, tempeh, tofu.

Now I live in a large house with one other person on four acres of land with eight garden beds. Then I lived in five rooms with four other people and two potted plants. Then I had a parakeet; now I have a canary. Then death was terrifying and infinitely distant. Now it is known: two parents, two good friends. Then I was scared of boys. Now I'm bored by most men my age. Then I yearned for romance. Now I know its greatness and ruin, and I cherish the steadiness of steadfast love.

Then there were penny loafers, patent-leather Mary Janes, and Keds. Now I have clogs, sandals, boots, and sneakers. Then I was shy and didn't say what I thought. Now I tell the truth as I see it, perhaps too readily. Then I wanted to write books; now I've written five. Then I relied on a body that was entirely cooperative and finely tuned. Now I live in one that, like my '97 Toyota, sometimes startles me with its signs of wear and tear. Then my hair was dark brown; now it's mostly white. Then I felt trapped. Now I feel almost too free to choose how to spend my days.

Then I had a foam-rubber pillow and slept alone in flannel pj's. Now I have two feather pillows and sleep in a white cotton nightgown beside my gentle husband. Then my mother dictated what I ate; now I have chocolate every day and bacon whenever I want. Then she made me dust the blinds and furniture every week; now I dust about once a month. Now, to get places, I walk, drive, or fly; then I walked or took buses or subways. Then I knew the rules; now I know there aren't any.

Then I was afraid of God. Now I pray to God daily to shelter me. Half the time I call God "her." Then it was always "him." Then everyone was "fine." Now people say what's wrong, try for the truth. Then the word cancer was rarely spoken. Now I hear it almost every week. Then I yearned to be noticed, to be seen. Now I take joy in the seeing. Look at the bark of that birch. Hear the spring water running down the hill. God! Bend over here and look at the dozens of tiny shadows cast by the setting sun.

Then I was a child. Now my children are

adults; I stare up at my son and marvel at the breadth of his shoulders. Then I told my mother nothing. Now my kids often tell me more than I want to know. Then life used me, propelled me, hastened me. Now I bow and walk toward something I still cannot name but see more clearly and know myself to be a part of, albeit a small, small part. Then I couldn't bear the thought of my not being, of a world without me. Now I often yearn for union with the ineffable, beyond any idea of me.

3.
The Object

A crow snatching up this resonant piece of my jewelry led me to run immediately to my desk.

PROMPT: Choose an object that is dear to you and write about your life experiences through the lens of this object—its history, what it represents, where it has traveled with you, how you may have lost it and in losing it, what else was lost. (Perhaps you will want, instead, to write about a "found object.")

Mezuzah

It's autumn, and I'm listening to Rickie Lee Jones sing "One Hand, One Heart" from *West Side Story* as I drive up Route 2, the sun in my eyes, my rose-tinted glasses giving the fall colors a make-over. And why not a bit of deception for a woman like me, a sucker for a raspy voice and sentimental Broadway lyrics such as these: "Make of our hands, one hand, / Make of our hearts, one heart"? Soon my eyes are wet, and I can barely see the view as Rickie Lee sings, "Now it begins, now we start; / One hand, one heart. / Even death won't part us now."

Yes, I see again that I'm a weepy Platonist longing for beauty, for the ideal, always hungry for essential union. I first heard this song sung by Tony and Maria in the wedding scene of *West Side Story* when I was a morose teenager, obsessed with ill-fated romance and the Holocaust. Right now, I'm not thinking about these two obsessions of my youth, but about my dead mother, and I don't want to revisit this grief because it's an old ache that has little to do with the actual Ruth and her faults. (Three years after her passing, I can still easily list them: critical, demanding, controlling.) All this colorful emotion today seems to have nothing to do with the ache for her, and the ache seems to have nothing to do with anything I can name. Yet, along with the old grief, there is a red sun rising within me—and that's about as far as I can get without telling you the story of the crow and the *mezuzah*.

When I was thirteen, my mother gave me a *mezuzah*, a tiny piece of parchment inscribed with a Jewish prayer and enclosed in a small case. Though traditionally attached to the front door post of Jewish homes, it can also be worn around the neck. The one my mother gave me was filigreed silver and very unlike the fancy-schmancy gold jewelry she usually insisted I wear. To my radical dismay, I liked it. It grew warm with the heat of my young body as I went around dreaming of better days. By "better days," I mean those that would include a handsome boy who adored me, a brilliant career in the ballet, and a trip on an ocean liner to France—or, at least, a trip away from our apartment in Queens: goofy Michael Epstein playing *Chopsticks* upstairs; my mother looking me up and down before school and insisting that I exchange my sneakers for "real shoes"; and the leaden presence of my father, stiff as one of those ventriloquist's dummies on tv. My father rarely spoke to me, unlike the handsome boy of my dreams, who found a seat next to mine on the ocean liner, read poetry aloud, and talked for days, mostly about me.

On the parchment scroll inside the case was printed the *Shema*, the holiest of all Jewish prayers. I'd prod the prayer scroll through the small opening in the back, making it dance up and down. I'd memorized the words in Hebrew school, so I didn't have to take it out and read them now: "Hear, O Israel, the Lord our God, the Lord is one." This monotheistic anthem of the ancient Jews is, I realize now, oddly akin to Tony and Maria's "Make of our hearts, one heart." This idea of oneness conveys to me a soft fusion, without thrusting or effort, an encompassing safety. If no one can separate you from the whole, then you can't be blamed, tagged, shot.

I wore the *mezuzah* intermittently as an adult, but returned to wearing it regularly during my mother's dying years. I bought a new chain for it with a foolproof lobster-claw catch, and it would sometimes hit my husband in the face when we made love. It lay cold and wet against my skin when I swam in the neighbor's pond, with tadpoles darting around me and the trees rising above, like strong hands holding up a heavy burden.

The prayer scroll had visibly browned and shrunk, but I could still see it through the small opening. As my mother traveled backward in time, her body contracting and her mind doing the odd tangos, foxtrots, and hokey-pokeys of dementia, the *mezuzah* stayed with me. I held it as I stared at her in bed. I wore it as I set down my grief on page after page and inadvertently began a book. The *mezuzah* was steadfast, like the wild apple tree entangled by grapevines outside my study window, like nature in all her manifestations. I found solace in my gardens, in the fact of grass and flowers, in how the earth supported my body as I knelt to work the soil or lay down on it to rest and breathed in its familiar, ancient smell.

When at last my mother died, I took the *mezuzah* off and placed it in a small, carved wooden box, which had replaced the large, black, fake-leather jewelry box she'd once bought me. I felt relief after her passing, and, happily, mystically, I seemed to find her in my gardens, in the tidy sky, in the untidy woods. I continued to hear her voice, softer now, but still advising me.

I finished my book, which was accepted by a small press. A friend asked if she could read it, then passed it on to a friend of hers who funds unusual projects. A few weeks later, that friend of a friend offered me a sizable grant to help publicize my book and get it into the world's hands. I discovered that the philanthropist's money had come from Holocaust reparations. I'd been born just as the camps were being liberated, so this gift felt like the completion of a circle, another layer in the healing of an unspeakable, and mysteriously personal, wound.

Oddly, I could no longer wear the *mezuzah*. I'd put it on, then quickly remove it. I asked a friend who was wise in such esoteric matters what to do. "Margaret," I said, "I can't wear it; it has bad energy or something." I explained how it was emotionally tied to my mother's long, hard death and to all other forms of Hebraic misery. "Is there any way to kind of 'clean' it? I'd like to wear it again."

Margaret suggested I take it outside in my yard and find a tree—"You'll know which one is right," she said—then put one end of the *mezuzah* in the earth under the tree and let the tree's roots "take the negativity out of it." I was to leave it there for twenty-four hours.

Her instructions reminded me of how, in our kosher home, when a fork meant for dairy was accidentally stabbed into a piece of chicken or meatloaf, Mom would stick the fork in the soil of a potted philodendron (the planter was in the shape of a donkey wearing a sombrero) and leave it there for twenty-four hours; according to Jewish law, this would purify the fork.

I found the "right" tree easily—a barren maple—then brushed aside the dry leaves at its base and placed my *mezuzah*, with its new chain and lobster-claw catch, partly in the ground. Then I went inside, wrote myself a note, and taped it to my desk as a reminder: "*Mezuzah* below maple behind garden with arrowwood border."

Twenty-four hours later, I walked slowly, almost ceremoniously, across the yard, found my tree, and looked down. The *mezuzah* was gone. I got down on my knees and pawed at the ground. Then I got a rake and combed the entire area. I got back down on my knees and ran my fingers though grass, dirt, and leaves. Nothing.

I ran into the house to tell my husband what had happened. After a long round of questions to make sure I hadn't simply forgotten where I'd put it, he said, "Crows like shiny things. Sometimes they put them in their nests."

Just then, a dark flock of crows flew noisily over our land.

"People underestimate crows," he added.

I went back outside and stood beside the tree under which my most treasured personal possession had been lost. I looked down at the ground and up at the sky. I thought of the crow plucking the *mezuzah* from the ground and spiriting it away, and, to my surprise, my sorrow began to lift. I moved from a state of dark panic to one of joy and freedom. I loved the idea of a bird flying sky-high, the silver chain hanging from its beak, the legacy of bondage, persecution, and grief taken up into a clear blue fall sky. It was nature, after all —the shiny fortress of the night sky, the earth with all her green indifference—that had comforted me during and after my mother's death. Surely, I owed it a gift in return.

4.

Family Relationships

This essay began with the wondrous words spoken to me by my niece, Kelsey, when we were swimming in the ocean together, Such words stay with you, and to assure that, I wrote them down as soon as I could. Soon after, a trip with my two grown kids was to about to begin. I followed my thoughts and feelings about this plan having no idea where it would lead, i.e., that the joy of being with Kelsey in the sea would contrast so sharply with our difficulties in the desert. (Please note how, as a writer, I also immediately recorded the words of the poem, which touched me when I was watching the movie.)

PROMPT: Write, in a freely associative manner, about your family at whatever point in time calls to you. If you have trouble entering this idea, write, "When I think of my family, I remember…." Repeat the phrase as many times as you need to until you arrive at a starting point.

O My Little Breath

Late-morning light falls on the gray carpet of our bedroom as I do my daily yoga practice and think about my upcoming trip with my two grown kids to the Southwest. I've been looking forward to it for months, but now, as the date draws near, I'm worried about how it will go. My children and I rarely travel together anymore. Were we taking this trip twenty years ago, Mara and Josh would be wide-eyed and happy just to be in a new place— much less Indian country. I remember them at two and four years old, gleefully running naked through our small apartment with long pieces of toilet paper stuck in their little butt cracks, their heads turned to watch their "tails" fly behind them.

Now I watch myself breathe, observing the roller coaster of thought, feeling, thought—the routine mind-ride of an adult. I know that in some ways the trip will be good: time with my children, wide vistas, dry air, a departure from the usual. I also know that it will be complex, traveling with two people who are so different from each other: Mara quiet, moody, and observant; Josh enthusiastic and extroverted. And me trying to keep them balanced.

Stretching my arms over my head and breathing deeply, I feel sad. I miss the thrill of anticipation I used to experience before traveling. Upstairs, my husband puts on a CD, and I hear folk singer John Gorka lament, "I'm sad and I'm angry/ armed with a broken heart." Bracing myself in the cobra pose, I wonder if that's it: if it's our broken hearts that steal from us the sensual joys of childhood and replace them with anxiety.

Then I remember last week, the joy of being in the warm salt water of the Atlantic with my ten-year-old niece, Kelsey. We were jumping the waves when she grabbed my shoulders and stuck her wet, tanned face, with her oversized new front teeth, about three inches from my own.

"Aunt Genie," she asked, "what are you?"

"What do you mean, honey?"

"I mean, what are you?"

A large wave was approaching. I grabbed her by the waist, and we jumped it. "I'm Jewish," I said.

"Then I'm Jewish, too," she said.

"Not really," I explained, "because your parents aren't. They're Catholic, so it's not in your blood. You and I are related through marriage— through love."

"What else are you?" Kelsey pressed. "Are you Irish?"

"No, I'm Russian and Polish and Austrian."

She gave me another of her toothy grins, and I kissed her cheek. Holding on to my hands and bobbing up and down, she kissed me back. "I love you," she said.

"And I love you," I said.

"And because I love you," she went on, her eyes locked to mine, "I'm Jewish and Russian and Polish and . . . what was that other thing?"

"Austrian," I said.

"And Austrian," she finished, nodding her head.

Oh, her unbroken heart, I thought. It's so simple—if I love you, then I am you.

A week after my morning of yoga and worry, I'm traveling with Mara and Josh in New Mexico. Entering Frijoles Canyon at Bandelier National Monument, we see a sign announcing that a ten-minute film about the Anasazi Indians is about to begin. "I don't want to see a movie," Mara says. "I'd rather be outside. I'll look for birds." She takes off with her binoculars.

As Josh and I find our seats in the dark, I think that Carl Jung was right: three is a terrible number to travel in; it's off balance and wants to become a more stable two or four.

Images of the excavated village that once thrived in this place appear on the screen, accompanied by reedy music and the deep, oily male voice that always narrates nature programs. "No one knows," the voice intones, "why they left their arable village center, where, on the canyon floor, they grew corn, beans, and squash." Then the screen fills with pictures of birds and small purple asters, and the voice begins to recite a Native American poem about the disappearance of animals, ceremony, ways of life: "O my little breath,

O my little heart," the poem goes, and I quickly reach into my pack for a pen and scribble the words on a napkin.

"That was really good," Josh says as we blink our way back into the daylight. Ahead of us stretches a long trail dotted with other visitors. Mara is nowhere to be seen. "I'll run back and get a guidebook," Josh says, "so we can follow the trail better." I watch him take off running with his long, dark legs, then go to look for his sister. I find her a short distance away, staring up a tree with her binoculars. She either doesn't hear me or else is ignoring me.

"See anything?" I ask.

"Nope, no birds," she says. "Just my luck."

I turn to look at the cave dwellings on the huge face of the canyon wall behind us. The rock glows pink in the fading afternoon light.

When Josh returns, we set out on the guided walk, and he reads enthusiastically from the small book at each stop. " 'Educational and religious ceremonies were performed here underground,' " he reads. "Can you imagine all those people living here? It's incredible."

"I think it's kind of boring," Mara says, kicking the dry earth.

The number three is working its bad voodoo. Josh's bright spirit is luring me from the darker light of his sister, and she knows it.

"I'm going ahead," Mara says.

"OK," I say. "We'll meet you soon."

Josh and I continue the guided walk as the sun sets and the cliff face turns a rich red. At the point where the trail snakes back toward the caves, we meet up with Mara, and the three of us begin climbing the narrow path up to the cave mouths. Beside a long, narrow opening in the rock, we hear an odd sound. Josh consults his guidebook. "A bat cave," he says.

"I knew that," Mara says, pointing. "Look there." Ever the quiet observer, she's already taken in the dark, powdery debris at the mouth of the cave. "Guano," she says.

We wait, hoping to see a bat fly out. When none does, we move on in silence.

We've gone only a few yards when Mara says

something curt, and I respond sharply, and she hisses at me, "I'm sick of how you talk to me."

"Not this again," Josh says. "I'm out of here, you guys." He walks ahead, while Mara and I stop dead in our tracks.

"Ever since Josh came," Mara says, "you've been nasty, you don't like anything I have to say, and you get all superficial and jumpy—just like him." She gives me another killer look.

I feel myself harden, my heart thrashing like a swimmer far out to sea, going down alone. "Go ahead," I snap. "Just go."

"Glad to," Mara says, slinging her binoculars over her shoulder and storming off.

I stand unmoving beside the opening to a cave, struggling to deal with my impossible feelings. It's not fair, I think, like a hurt child. I'm losing the battle and sinking, and I don't know what to do but turn to stone, get heavier and just drown. Fuck it.

Trying to breathe, I look down at my feet, and the words of the Native American poem return to me: *O my little breath, O my little heart.* I reach into my pack for the napkin to see if I have them right. Then I slowly repeat them to myself, straighten my back, and let my breath enter. I put my hand to my chest and feel my heart drumming. The sun has dropped behind the hill. *O my little breath.* I take a deeper breath, then another, and I begin to soften and sense an exit. It's ok, little heart. A bat flaps its black wings above my head, and I watch it fly off.

Continuing on, I see Josh up ahead, climbing a ladder to the highest cliff dwelling, and Mara standing at its base, looking up. I walk over and put my arms around her. "I'm sorry," I say. "I know it's hard. Yes, it's different with Josh. I understand." I press her thin body to my own. "Let's forget it. Let's just forget it. I love you."

Mara turns to me—*O my little heart*—and says, "OK, we'll start over."

And I say, "Yes, we'll start over."

And in this place where the soil is bone-dry and the ghosts of the exiled are everywhere, where I can't imagine anything starting over, we do.

5.
In-Depth Focus
Upon One Experience

This essay came from an assignment I gave to my writing workshop members.

PROMPT: Read "Dressing Her." Slow time down as much as possible and pay absolute attention to what unfolds during that period. This, of course, requires the inclusion of far more details than are usually present in a piece of writing and develops our ability to see; seeing, in every sense, is inextricably bound to the art of writing.

Dressing Her

I sit on the pale blue rug near her feet as she lies back in the recliner, which her husband, Frank, has just bought so she's able to rest and sleep in the living room. She is looking at me from behind the stylish, rimless glasses which she'd recently bought after I chided her for years about her clunky old ones. Thin oxygen tubes are set in her nostrils and hitched together under her chin to become one larger tube resembling an odd umbilicus snaking to a green tank which hisses at regular intervals.

"Are you okay sitting down there?" she asks. "Oh, Rob," I say, "you know I always like sitting on the floor." I throw her a kiss as she nods slowly; everything is slow now, and as she slowly smiles, a soft glow comes to me from her eyes, which are brown and often aimed down on the lower half of her bi-focals so she can see us up close, the better to assess and care for us, an exacting aide and advisor for all manner of things, from medical advice to movie and book reviews, to restaurants, to life's recurrent dilemmas.

When we first met, she was shy. I was her new writing teacher recommended by a therapist whom she'd been seeing because of problems with a stepson who'd moved in with her and her husband. Robyn was obviously thrilled to be writing after a long hiatus, but during our initial conference, I could barely get a word out of her. Over time, however, her jaw unhinged, as did mine, and we found that we had far more than our birthdays in common. She told me that she'd written two novels and then, after a few months of writing in my workshop, she announced that she'd decided they were "too Victorian and insipid." A week later, she burned them. I own a photo of her stuffing them into a woodstove. Never having read them, I've often wondered if they had merit, which Robyn might have been blind to owing to her perfectionism. Perfectionism can lead to dismissal.

As time passed, I came to understand that Robyn's need to tend to others was born of having taken on early the responsibility of bolstering her depressed mother. This way of being also made it sometimes difficult to feel close to her because it was so damn hard to get her to say what she wanted. Nonetheless, our friendship happily pushed beyond her idealization of me as a published writer and mentor, and ballooned into discussions and disclosures of all manner of things, I mean all, and thereby I came down to size as a close friend to talk with. And that's how I remember Robyn best, talking, before the cancer, when we'd meet on Mondays for our long walks up on my hill. She'd exit her always spiffy clean silver Tercel, I'd meet her in our entryway, she'd look down to examine me, we'd hug and I'd feel the cushiony softness of her breasts. Then we'd take off down the road. For two years, during which my Mom was dying in a nearby nursing home and I was a wreck, we had a deal: I talked about my upset for as long as I needed, and she simply listened. Then it was her turn and she'd give me her weekly update, which often included a detailed description of her discontent with her job as well as an extensive catalogue of what she and her husband had eaten that week-end. The menu was boring, but it was Robyn.

Years later, after eighteen months of life with lung cancer, when she could barely walk, I plodded beside her, her arm looped though mine, the portable oxygen tank hanging from her shoulder. We inched our way down Newell Pond Road to the corner and back and she, who loved to talk, barely talked, and the sky was bright above us, and the pavement hard below us and we moved through the giving air until she had to stop to gather enough strength to go on.

At last, back at her house, I helped her up the two front steps, then opened the door as she puffed and apologized for puffing between her labored breaths. "Rob," I said, hugging her carefully," quit it." As she began to sit down, I remembered how, a few years before, I'd seen her at our local co-op where she was having lunch with a friend as I was rushing about trying to find something edible for a plane ride to California. She waved to me and I ran to her table, where she put her sandwich down and looked at me with a love that was almost fearsome, a love I tried to feed back to her full force during her illness, a love I still can, from time to time, summon at will.

She and I had plans to become old ladies together. Frank, who was fifteen years her senior, would have died and she would be living in a small apartment in Northampton, one filled with, perhaps, a quarter of what cluttered her home. Of all her things, I knew for sure she'd keep the handmade little bird box painted blue with the tiniest hole for a phantom bird to fly in and out of freely. She loved birds and butterflies, knew their names, and always had to stop, look and exclaim whenever she saw one.

A few weeks before the end, I arrived one day and opened the door without knocking so as not to awaken her, but she heard me, opened her eyes, smiled, stared at me and, ever the accommodating host, began to get up. "I'm coming," I said," just stay there, okay Rob?" She shut her eyes and nodded. Her hair was almost entirely absent, that thick curly black mass gone, leaving only random strands, leaving her so reduced. She looked at me hard again, then lifted the wooden handle on the side of the chair, which loosened its position from back to forward. She turned toward me, her eyes moving up and down my body, "You look so nice, I have to look nice too." As she moved further forward readying herself to stand, I moved quickly beside her, placed my hand gently on her arm and said, "Rob, I had to dress up for that writer's union conference, but you're just here and you look fine, really." She stared at me. "And we're not going anywhere," I continued, "we're staying right here." But she kept pressing forward as my hand dropped from her arm to curl firmly around her elbow and help her stand as she called "Frank, Frank . . ." until he came. As I stood beside her untangling the tube on her arm, he asked, "What is it?"

"Frank," she pleaded, she whom I'd never heard plead for anything in all the fifteen years I knew her, "I have to change my clothes, I have to." As I watched, I recalled how Robyn never really gave a damn about clothing, how she'd buy four of the same tops in different colors at J.C. Penney, how she didn't own one skirt, one dress. It was more than the morphine, I thought and wondered if it was in order to span the gap between me, the healthy one, and her, the very ill; or was it her devotion to propriety, to always doing the right thing again? Was it her lingering unconscious wish to still be a real writer who went to a real conference for writers?

"But," Frank said, "it took us so long to get you dressed and you look fine, you really do, no kidding, Honey." He leaned in so they were face to face. "You look fine and you're comfortable, right?"

"No," she insisted, "I have to change. Please, please," and she made the "e" long as the oxygen still kept up its hissing in the background.

"But," he tried again as I stood to the side, wishing I'd worn sweat pants and the rattiest t-shirt I had instead of my silk black pants, finely tapered lime green shirt and pearls. "Please honey please," and so slowly, Frank on one side and me on the other, we ferried Robyn into the bedroom where, exhausted, she plopped down on the edge of the bed. Above the headboard I took another look at Jesus, Buddha, a large Jewish star, plus a plastic saint or two, anyone, spirit or thing we'd found that might turn her face, that pale oval, back in the direction of life.

"Okay," Frank said, "what will it be?"

"Oh, I don't know yet," I heard her say as I stared at her closet, which was beyond belief neat with piles of clothing, each stack perfectly aligned, like the bottles of pills on the kitchen table, the tidy list of medications, and notations of the times they were to be taken. Before the cancer, Robyn had been the quality assurance person at our local Visiting Nurses Association. Her kitchen cupboards, with their highly organized, abundant larder, had always put mine to shame.

The last novel she'd been writing, displayed the same exactness—*The Good Woman*,a futuristic account of an old woman roaming the remains of what had once been the United States. As she traveled, she'd come upon small enclaves of survivors whom she tried to assist in one way or another. Robyn was halfway through revising it when cancer came and writing left and with it her fierce ambition, augmented by the interest of an agent. Every week she had spent her entire Fridays, days off from her regular job, working eight hours on the novel. When, at my request, she gave me a chapter to read, there was not the slightest technical error. I honestly praised her writing, praise which she often dismissed.

After she'd worked hard on the book for two years or so, I was given the first entire draft to read and liked its original visionary angle, its rather quirky protagonist and the equally quirky characters she came upon, some of whom were quite violent, so unlike their creator. Robyn never had a child, but she created one in her book, a lovable girl of ten who was looking for her mother. After a second draft, when she could no longer climb the stairs to her writing room and computer, she offered me what had been completed, and made me promise not to ever try to have it published. It now sits in a white box on a shelf in my office.

Frank pulled out a pair of red sweatpants. "These okay?" Robyn looked up slowly, then shook her head. "How about these," he asked, "black, like Genie's?" She nodded her assent. "Now we'll have to get the gray ones off," and he and I kneeled before her and gently managed each leg, rolling down the material slowly, then slowly putting one black pant leg on, then another, pulling them over her thin white skin which could no longer mask green veins and blue, "Lift your leg honey, can you?" he asked and she shut her eyes with the effort. She took a deep gurgling breath and then, "my shirt," she whispered, and I went to the closet and carefully lifted a white one. She raised her head to see, then shook it slowly. No. She was not smiling; she was all effort and intention as I held up a plain green turtle neck and said, "This one is nice," and she again slowly shook her head. I looked down at her, her head hanging until Frank said, "Rob, this is it," as he extracted a bright yellow shirt from the bottom of the pile and she looked slowly up, said nothing. Then carefully, first removing the tubes from her nostrils, we took off her navy shirt, arm by arm, then lifted each and wended her hand and arm through until she was set and she nodded and Frank reattached the tubing. "Ready?" he asked, she nodded again, and the two of us lifted her to standing and walked her back through the small hallway to her chair.

"Turn around," Frank said, helping her so that her back faced the chair. "Now," he said, holding her on both sides, "sit down." Slowly she did, then she closed her eyes for a few minutes as Frank left for the kitchen, and I sat down again in my usual spot on the floor, looking up at her, waiting. A few minutes later, Robyn opened her eyes with surprise that I was there. She smiled and slowly said, "I love you." "I love you too," I said, "and I'm so sorry I came here all dressed up, I promise I won't do that ever again." But she didn't seem to understand, she just kept looking at me, looking with her soft eyes as I sat and gently patted her leg over and over looking at her because I knew I'd not be doing this for very long. It was not much longer.

In the last of the e-mails she sent to friends chronicling her illness, she'd written, "I'm very tired and so wishing you all the love and luck in the world, and there's a lot of it, by gum! I guess that's it." Robyn.

6.

Life Passages

As one reaches the age of sixty, mortality becomes a predominant issue for many of us, particularly if one loses a good friend. This was my subject— aging and its losses and, more importantly, the loss of Robyn Oughton. The end of the essay, the description of my husband and me seeing and hearing Wynton Marsalis felt like just the right ending, a chronology I'd never imagine would work. But which did. It was what happened.

PROMPT: Read "20, 40, 60, 80," then write about aging, focusing on whatever stage of life calls to you the most strongly.

20, 40, 60, 80

Iunabashedly confess that I do not relish aging as I quickly close in on sixty. I can't believe that number, how life's waters, pure and rushing, have so mysteriously and abruptly carried me here, how the moon keeps on with its rhythms of full and thin and three days of gone. How the sun rises and falls, the days passing faster and faster as I use up my breath and move toward death. I think: twenty, forty, sixty, eighty. Both my parents died when they were eighty; I think seventy-five percent of my life is probably gone. I ask, "Where did it go?"

I remember once walking in Boston with my son along the harbor near a famous fish restaurant. I can't remember the name of the place, another thing about aging: "What was that woman's name?" "Who just called me?" "What did I come into this room for?" "What the hell is going on?" Oh, yes, I was walking with my son near that famous restaurant. I was about thirty-five, he was ten and as a humongous red truck passed us, the driver stuck his head out the window and whistled enthusiastically at me, some "hubba-hubba" kind of thing. What was I wearing? Probably a mini-skirt. How was my hair? Probably long and dark and parted down the middle. As the exhaust briefly whirled around us, Josh muttered, "I can't believe that jerk, I wish I could slam him one."

I was touched by my son's chivalrous impulse, amused by his alleged need to defend me; I was also annoyed and flattered by the dumb-ass trucker who'd hoot at a woman with her son clearly in tow. Was Josh upset by his mother's sexuality? Was it some Oedipal thing? I have no idea, but I remember the scene well.

Now I'm mostly invisible to guys, unless they're seventy or over. "I don't feel that at all," one woman, my age, replied when I mentioned this phenomenon. "I never was noticed," she said, "it's you pretty ones who get to suffer this time."

Recently we went to Bishop's Lounge, a bar, to listen to jazz. The place was smoke-clogged and jammed, our drinks long in coming when our friend, Michael, whispered loudly, "There's so and so and nodded toward a shlumped over, very famous writer in a trench coat, who was slowly moving toward the bar. The writer found a stool, took off his coat and sat on it. He lit a cigarette, was quickly handed a beer by a plump young bartender and began to stare rather icily at me as I scrunched next to my husband in a paltry attitude of defense. I was, I confess, vaguely flattered because it was that famous writer and his rheumy eyes made me see myself in a more literary fashion. But God, he was old, and I didn't like the attention of such an antique creature.

How can one accept, no less enjoy, aging in a time and place where god is twenty-five, where TV and magazine advertisements show twenty or thirty something's in halter tops or tight t-shirts and the only time there's a lined face framed by white hair is when it's an ad for incontinence, high blood pressure, or cholesterol. What about wisdom? Endurance? What about the beauty of a face etched with the documentation of survival through years that include dollops of suffering. Show me anyone over fifty who has not known tragedy and I'll show you Icarus just about to lose his wings as they melt under the pressure of a hot sun before he plunges into the sea. Maybe angels will arrive, maybe a Med Evac, a shark, a mermaid, maybe death.

So here I am walking down the only real long corridor there is, trudging at times, sometimes wanting to sing and dance, but often whining as I'm pushed from behind by my two dead parents encouraging, "It's fine, it's fine," and a thirty-five year old daughter saying, "You're young, you can't die Mom, I love you, you're my hero and if you die I'll never get over it."

But it's not death that's the devil, it's the body and my fear of the kind of deterioration my own mother faced in her long years of decline with Parkinson's and dementia. Recently we've bought long-term care insurance to circumvent nursing home hell. Recently three friends were diagnosed with cancer, one of them my best. At last, we've written our wills. My husband is thirteen years younger than I am and going along a bit early for the ride. "Why the hell don't you catch up?" I sometimes yell at him, "C'mon!" He smiles and is silent. What can he say? So far as I know, there are no aging pills on the market, no happy senior citizens touting wrinkle promotion or organ deterioration syrup. And so I hold my husband, and he holds me, and, alone, I hold what life I have left in my arms like a child, trying to comfort it, love it, make it laugh. I think I can, I think I can, but sometimes it feels like a real job, not like living as a three-year-old. How many times does three go into sixty? Too many.

"Oh, you're young," Gordon, the eighty-year-old man I like to sit next to in synagogue says to me. When he says this, I have no idea what to do. Sing *Hallelujah*? Say *Amen*? Thank God for the good life I've had? Gordon is a beautiful old soul with the face of a kindly god. When he smiles, his face says "Love." Sometimes I feel an impulse to sidle up to him, thigh to thigh, caress his chin, turn that face to me and kiss him hard on the lips, but I'm afraid I'll give him a heart attack.

I had no fear whatsoever of kissing my friend the closest of my friends, Robyn who, at fifty-four, was ridden with cancer that started in her lungs and then spread just about everywhere after two years of chemo hell, the details of which I heard almost daily. We often held hands, and said our "I love you's" above the racket of her three parakeets.

During her illness, I sat and stood and laughed and wept and did as many things for her as she would allow. The last time I took her to do errands—the drugstore, the pet store, the market—she marveled, "Oh my God, Genie, you can just get up and go and do all that. It's amazing. Do you have any idea?" I stopped for a second behind the steering wheel before I started the engine and considered this; it was hard. Then I took her home, helped her change from a portable oxygen tank to the huge tank in her living room, kissed her good-bye, once on each cheek, got back into the car, and drove again past the familiar landscapes I could barely imagine existing without the accompaniment of her voice.

How many times did we say good-bye? Far more than sixty before she died. I want to say "passed away." It sounds nicer. But she died, and I keep wondering where she is, although I've visited her gravesite twice, although I could swear she was in the barred owl that flew over my head in the woods a month after her death and then sat about twenty feet from me on a tree and stared. I hadn't seen a barred owl for seven years, since the winter preceding my mother's death when one came and sat outside our kitchen window week after week, storm after storm. But there it was, and there was I, my heart fractured by Robyn's departure. I stared back at it and began crying, grabbing tissues out of my jacket pocket, snuffling loudly. It watched and watched me, taking my grief into its black eyes. I could swear it was Robyn visiting me for comfort; or God in the form of a bird; I couldn't swear a thing. Then off it flew, and I walked back home.

"What does it feel like to lose a good friend?" someone in her forties asked me. I'm lucky, I thought, to have come this far before being able to answer this question. It feels hard and empty. What I didn't say was that sometimes beneath this hard emptiness there is a sense of flight, wings spread, chest and heart holding more love with Robyn inside me, with the knowledge that my heart won't ever seal up as tight ever again, with the earned real understanding that we all are dying. I've already been blessed with six more years than she had.

When Robyn and I walked down the street together talking, I never noticed who looked at either of us. I didn't care, and Robyn helped me not care with her weird, bulky winter hats, and, later, the little red or purple caps she wore to cover her baldness.

The middle-aged crease, shrink, fade, and, if lucky, become grateful "beholders," slowly losing the desire to be noticed, like the taste for Necco Wafers or Pez. I'm slowly replacing that desire to be seen with that of seeing—the faces of those I love, children, the sky, clouds, the cardinal in the bush, strangers, the socks of that woman with MS who swims at the Y. "Great socks," I say as I change for my workout. "Yes," she says, "Now that I'm older, I'm going for wilder, especially in the sock department." I think briefly of Robyn's strange hats, look at this woman and think "old," and then, as we continue talking, she says she's fifty-eight and can't wait to turn sixty. God, I can't believe she's younger than I am I think as I go off to blow dry my hair so it won't fall flat.

When I return to my locker after my work out, I notice no one is left in the locker room, the one in which Robyn and I met three times every week, every winter for twelve years. I look in the mirror, arrange my hair again, then walk to the closet to retrieve my coat. Grief suddenly hits again—it's like walking by the sea and out of nowhere a wave breaks over you. I begin crying as I pack up my things and walk past a few people, averting my wet face, and then I'm out the door heading toward my car. Outside the sky is pink with sunset. I stand and stare at it over the red and white Toyota sign and the bare November trees. Beauty and pain are sisters, I think. Robyn and I are sisters. Aging and death are sisters. I can't see Robyn as she was, but I see something akin to her in birds and sky. The part of me that will never die, the soul, is invisible, but I wonder if I will always miss, even just a little, the young woman who, walking down streets, drew stares from strangers

A few weeks before Robyn's death, my husband and I went to see Wynton Marsalis perform at a small club in Northampton, Massachusetts, called the Iron Horse. Bill and I sat about four feet from Marsalis, and Bill, who loves music more than he loves me (he might deny that), more than life itself (perhaps that he would not deny), was entranced, transported, lost from his body and found in pure sound—like the light into which prophets and poets claim we omit "will" ecstatically dissolve into at the end. I kept looking at him. He's a serious guy, not quick with a smile, not easy with words, which he respects too much too misuse. But maybe it's just the Ohio in him. In any case, he's aware of their often paltry ability to hold truth, unlike the long note from Wynton's trumpet, that sound emitted from a gleaming piece of metal, its mouthpiece surrounded by those wide lips and cheeks, face muscles, like circus performers, triple-jointed, miraculous. As I looked at Bill, took in his strong, erect body, I felt his spirit undulating above it, utterly lost to flesh. Then the blue of his eyes caught the brown of mine for a second,, and he leaned toward me and whispered, "I could die now." My own eyes moistened at his joy, and I wanted so badly to believe that his joy was what came for Robyn, a portent of what comes for us all in the end.

The Author

Genie Zeiger's memoir, *How I Find Her: A Mother's Dying and a Daughter's Life*, was released in May 2001 by Sherman Asher Publishing of Santa Fe. After being highly praised in *"O,"* Oprah's magazine, *Hadassah Magazine*, and by many other reviewers, it is now in its second printing. It was also published in Germany by Kindler-Verlag in the spring of 2003.

Her second memoir, *"Atta Girl"* was published in 2005.

Zeiger, a frequent commentator for NPR, including *All Things Considered*, is also the recipient of a Massachusetts Cultural Council award for poetry. She has published three collections of poems, *Sudden Dancing*, (A.W.A. Press),*Leaving Egypt* and *Radio Waves*, (White Pine Press). She is a creative writing workshop leader in Shelburne, and the poetry editor for *Sanctuary*, Massachusetts' Audubon's magazine. A regular contributor to *The Sun*, her poems, stories and personal essays have also appeared in dozens of magazines including *The New York Times Book Review, The Massachusetts Review, The Georgia Review*, and *Tikkun.*

Companions for the Journey Series

Inspirational work by well-known writers in a small-book format
designed to be carried along on your journey through life.

Volume 21
What Happened Was . . .
On Writing Personal Essay and Memoir
Genie Zeiger
978-935210-04-7   106 PAGES $15.00

Volume 20
Mountain Tasting
Haiku and Journals of Santoka Taneda
Translated by John Stevens
978-1-935210-03-0   200 PAGES $16.00

Volume 19
Between the Floating Mist
Poems of Ryokan
Translated by Hide Oshiro and Dennis Maloney
978-1-935210-05-4   90 PAGES $14.00

Volume 18
Breaking the Willow
Poems of Parting, Exile, Separation and Return
Translated by David Lunde
978-1-893996-95-3   96 PAGES $14.00

Volume 2

There Is No Road: Proverbs by Antonio Machado

Translated by Mary G. Berg and Dennis Maloney

1-893996-66-2   118 PAGES $14.00

Volume I

Wild Ways: Zen Poems of Ikkyu

Translated by John Stevens

1-893996-65-4   152 PAGES $14.00